SOUTHEAST ASIANS

**Rice plant
important source
of Southeast Asian food**

IMMIGRATION AND THE AMERICAN WAY OF LIFE

Geologically speaking, the continent of North America is very old. The people who live here, by comparison, are new arrivals. Even the first settlers, the American Indians who came here from Asia about 35,000 years ago, are fairly new, not to speak of the first European settlers who came by ship or the refugees who flew in yesterday. Whenever they came, they were all immigrants. How all these immigrants live together today to form one society has been compared to the making of a mosaic. A mosaic is a picture formed from many different pieces. Thus, in America, many groups of people—from African Americans or Albanians to Tibetans or Welsh—live side by side. This human mosaic was put together by the immigrants themselves, with courage, hard work, and luck. Each group of immigrants has its own history and its own reasons for coming to America. Immigrants from different regions have their own way of creating communities for themselves and their children. In creating those communities, they not only keep elements of their own heritage alive but also enrich further the fabric of American society. Each book in *Recent American Immigrants* will examine a part of this human mosaic up close. The books will look at some of the most recent arrivals to find out what they are like and how they fit into the whole mosaic.

Recent American Immigrants

SOUTHEAST ASIANS

William
McGuire

Consultant
Roger Daniels, Department of History
University of Cincinnati

Franklin Watts

New York • London • Toronto • Sydn

Developed by: Ω **Visual Education Corporation**
Princeton, NJ

Maps: Patricia R. Isaacs/Parrot Graphics

Cover photograph: © Michael Douglas/The Image Works

Photo Credits: p. 3 (L) Mark Downey; p. 3 (M) Sharon Chester/
Comstock; p. 3 (R) Mark Downey; p. 9 James R. Smith/Globe Photos;
p. 10 John Robaton/Leo de Wys, Inc.; p. 11 (L) Craig Aurness/Woodfin
Camp & Associates, Inc.; p. 11 (R) Leo Touchet/Woodfin Camp &
Associates, Inc.; p. 13 Globe Photos; p. 14 Joe Viesti/Viesti Associates,
Inc.; p. 14 (inset) Courtesy of the United Nations; p. 16 Courtesy of the
Vietnam News Agency, Hanoi; p. 18 UPI/Bettmann Newsphotos; p. 22
(T) AP/Wide World Photos; p. 22 (M) UPI/Bettmann Newsphotos;
p. 22 (B) UPI/Bettmann Newsphotos; p. 23 (T) Reuters/Bettmann;
p. 23 (M) AP/Wide World Photos; p. 23 (B) Gamma-Liaison; p. 27
Courtesy of Dith Pran; p. 28 Magnus Bartlett/Woodfin Camp &
Associates, Inc.; p. 30 Courtesy of the United Nations High
Commissioner for Refugees; p. 33 David Burnett/Contact Press
Images; p. 39 (T) Courtesy of the United Nations High Commissioner
for Refugees; p. 39 (B) Courtesy of the United Nations High
Commissioner for Refugees; p. 40 AP/Wide World Photos; p. 43
Courtesy of the Cambodian Buddhist Society; p. 47 John Fitzhugh/The
Sun Herald; p. 49 Courtesy of the United Nations High Commissioner
for Refugees; p. 51 Herman J. Kokojan/Black Star; p. 55 Courtesy of
the United Nations; p. 57 Courtesy of the John Michael Kohler Arts
Center; p. 58 Richard Haynes; p. 61 Bob Daemmrich.

Library of Congress Cataloging-in-Publication Data

McGuire, William.
Southeast Asians / William McGuire.
p.   cm. — (Recent American immigrants)
Includes bibliographical references and index.
Summary: Describes how refugees from Vietnam, Cambodia, and Laos
have struggled to build new lives in America and preserve their cultural
heritage after escaping war and repression in their homelands.
ISBN 0-531-11108-3
1. Indochinese Americans — Juvenile literature. 2. United States
—Emigration and immigration — Juvenile literature. 3. Indochina
—Emigration and immigration — Juvenile literature. [1. Indochinese
Americans. 2. United States — Emigration and immigration.]
I. Title. II. Series.
E184.I43M34   1991
973'.049922 — dc20   90-12996 CIP AC

Contents

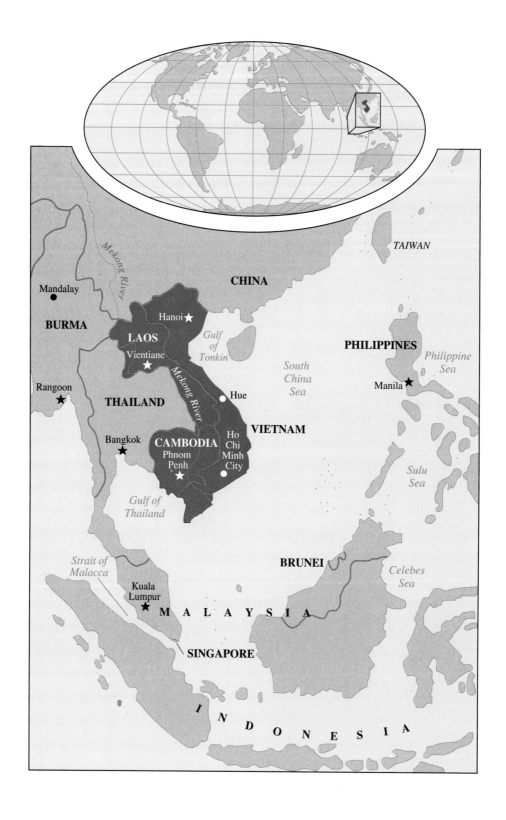

TAIWAN

CHINA

Mandalay

Hanoi ★

BURMA

LAOS

Gulf
of
Tonkin

PHILIPPINES

Philippine
Sea

Vientiane
★

Mekong River

South
China
Sea

Rangoon
★

THAILAND

Manila ★

Hue

VIETNAM

Bangkok
★

CAMBODIA

Ho
Chi
Minh
City

Phnom
Penh
★

Sulu
Sea

Gulf of
Thailand

BRUNEI

Celebes
Sea

Strait of
Malacca

Kuala
Lumpur
★ M A L A Y S I A

SINGAPORE

I N D O N E S I A

Mekong River

Southeast Asia: Three Troubled Countries

In the tropical region we call "Southeast Asia," there are ten countries, though in our book we are concerned with only three of them—Vietnam, Cambodia, and Laos. By the end of 1990, more than 1 million people will have fled to the United States from those three countries, seeking refuge from the war, persecution, and violence that have come to their homelands.

The area of Southeast Asia is more than half the size of our mainland forty-eight states. It has a population of nearly 442 million. It is made up of two long peninsulas that jut to the south from China and India, and many islands further south and east. The Malay Peninsula contains parts of Burma (now called Myanmar), Thailand (formerly called Siam), and Malaysia, and the city-state of Singapore. The island countries include Indonesia, another part of Malaysia, Brunei, and the Philippines. The Indochina peninsula contains Vietnam, Laos, Cambodia, and part of Thailand. Only Thailand has kept its independence through the years. All the other countries were owned by foreign countries for many years: Burma and Malaysia by the British, Indonesia by the Dutch, the Philippines by the Spanish (and the Americans), and Vietnam, Laos, and Cambodia by the French. They all have become independent since World War II, which ended in 1945.

In the peninsular countries there are rugged mountains and tropical rain forests, and the valleys are drained by great rivers, like the Mekong. The animal life includes elephants, tigers, crocodiles, snakes, and many kinds of monkeys. The people live mostly in villages in the lowlands, where rice is the main crop. There are not many big cities. This region has such a variety of peoples, languages, and cultures that it is hard to make statements that apply to everyone. The people show in their culture the influence of China and of India, where the dominant religion, Buddhism, came from. Roman Catholicism and Islam (dominant in Indonesia) also have followers, as well as Confucianism and Taoism from China. And there are tribes in the mountains that hold to simple beliefs that are called "animism."

VIETNAM

Vietnam, about the size of New Mexico, is the largest of the three countries and the one best known to us. It winds like the letter "S" along the South China Sea for more than a thousand miles. At its narrowest, Vietnam is no more than fifty miles wide. Its people are a blend of Chinese, Thai, and Indonesian. The Chinese, who ruled the Vietnamese for a thousand years, taught them about science and literature. The Vietnamese became a well-educated people. Their Buddhism was colored by Confucianism from China. But in the remote mountain areas, peoples lived, and still do, who are little touched by civilization. In the deltas of the Red River in the north and the Mekong in the south are sweeping stretches of rice paddies.

LAOS

Laos is also a long, narrow country, coiled along the west side of Vietnam. Of the countries of this region, it is the least touched by modern civilization. It is landlocked and mountainous, and its great river, the Mekong, has rapids and falls that

Xai Loi Buddhist temple in Ho Chi Minh City (formerly Saigon), Vietnam

make ship transport difficult. Most of the Laotians live in the valley of the Mekong River. The Mekong rises in China, runs through northern Laos, then forms the boundary with Thailand. Then it flows through lowlands in the South on its way to Cambodia.

The dominant people in the South, the Lao, are related to the Thai. Both may have migrated from China in the distant past. Three hundred years ago the Lao had a powerful kingdom that ruled much of the region. In the northern highlands, tribespeople called "Hmong" also came from

A remote mountain village in Laos

China in the early 1800s. Their villages, often hidden in the jungle, are scattered across Laos, Vietnam, and Thailand. They are mostly animist, but some are Buddhist. They believe in magic spells and evil spirits. Until recently the Hmong had no written language.

CAMBODIA

The Mekong flows on through the saucerlike lowlands of Cambodia, whose people are called "Khmers." They too are Buddhist. (For a few years, recently, the country took an old name, "Kampuchea," but it is again called "Cambodia.") More than a thousand years ago, the Khmers ruled an empire that covered much of the region, including Laos and southern Vietnam. The Khmer kings, influenced by the art and religion of India, built imposing temples and palaces at their capital, Angkor, far inland. Wonderful stone sculptures, showing both Hindu and Buddhist gods, decorated the buildings. The most famous temples are Angkor Wat and Angkor Thom. (In the Khmer language, *angkor* means "capital," *wat* means "temple," and *thom* means "big.") After the empire declined, the jungle took over Angkor, and the capital was moved to Phnom Penh. Angkor was found again, by French explorers, only in the nineteenth century. The Cambodians worked with the French to restore Angkor. They are very proud of this great work of their ancestors, one of the wonders of the world.

The Khmers Meet the West

In the late 1500s, a Cambodian king, Satha, was at war with the Thais. He heard of white men in ships on his coast. They were Spaniards, who had conquered the Philippines. Satha asked for their help. Hoping for gold and adventure, an expedition of Spaniards arrived. They killed Satha and his son, looted the palace at Phnom Penh, and put a new king on the throne. For several years, the Spanish abused the Cambodians. Finally, some of the Khmer nobles had enough. They rose up and massacred all the Spanish in their quarters. The Cambodians had no more visits from Europeans until the nineteenth century.

Source: Adapted from Claudia Canesso, *Cambodia* (New York: Chelsea, 1989), p. 37.

Angkor Wat in Cambodia

THE ETHNIC CHINESE

Over the centuries, the Southeast Asian countries have constantly been involved with China, their powerful neighbor to the north. The Chinese from time to time invaded the region. But other times they came peacefully, as merchants. In this way millions of Chinese migrated to other Asian countries, perhaps 8 or 9 million in this region, in search of opportunity. They are known as "overseas Chinese" or "ethnic Chinese." The Chinese merchants settled mainly in the towns. They had their own neighborhoods ("Chinatowns") and retained their own customs, language, and religion. Vietnam had the largest number of ethnic Chinese of any country. Because the Chinese kept to themselves and were often prosperous, some of the Vietnamese, Cambodians, and Laotians felt suspicious and unfriendly toward them.

EUROPEANS IN SOUTHEAST ASIA

The Spanish came to the region in the sixteenth century and conquered the Philippines but failed to get a foothold in Cambodia. Trading ships also came to the Indochinese coast from France, England, and Holland. They exchanged European goods for spices, tea, and other products. By the seventeenth century the first Catholic missionaries arrived in southern Vietnam and spread through the region. They were mainly Jesuit and Dominican priests from France. The priests made many converts, particularly in southern Vietnam, and they did much to help the people. They established schools and introduced a written alphabet for the Vietnamese language, using letters as in western European countries. They taught French and introduced European ideas that were sometimes difficult for the Vietnamese to understand. They also encountered some hostility.

The French Invade   The French had won trading rights from the Vietnamese as early as the 1780s and felt they had a privileged position. In 1861, they landed troops in Saigon, a large Vietnamese city, claiming that they had to protect the Christians, both lay people and priests. After capturing the city, the French gradually took control of Vietnam and Cambodia. They established garrisons and forts and took over the plantations where rice and rubber trees grew. The local kings were allowed to reign, though with little real power. The French army and administrators were the actual rulers. In 1887, France formed a union called "French Indochina," to which Laos was added soon afterward.

The French Influence   Undoubtedly the French brought some benefits to its possession. The schools started by the priests continued, and many people got French educations.

The French brought Catholicism to Southeast Asia in the seventeenth century. Here, a buffalo cart passes in front of the church at Savannakhet, Laos.

But because the schools favored the Christians, there was a drop in the general literacy rate. The French brought technical knowledge, built railroads and seaports, and encouraged commerce. French scholars made studies of the people, their languages, history, and arts. But the French treated the people as inferiors and exploited and neglected them. They were

A field of opium poppies

discriminated against in business, social life, and the schools. And the French encouraged the growing of poppies, especially in the mountain areas, to produce opium. Though opium has medical uses and is therefore of commercial importance, its use can become a habit, or addiction. Strong addictive drugs, such as heroin, can be made from opium. The French shut their eyes to drug traffic in opium, because it was profitable.

THE JAPANESE OCCUPATION

During the 1930s, Japan was seeking to take over the mainland of east Asia. They invaded China and fought there until 1945, killing millions of Chinese people. In 1940 they moved into the northern part of French Indochina. They told the people of the Asian countries that they should get rid of European influence and domination. The Vietnamese at first welcomed the Japanese, but soon they found them as cruel as the French, or worse. In the summer of 1941, the Japanese took over the rest of Indochina. Then came war between Japan and the Allies, including the United States. The Japanese took most of the crops to feed their troops, and thousands of Vietnamese died of starvation. The French were finally thrown out altogether, and the Japanese set up as puppet emperor a Vietnamese prince, Bao Dai.

Many Vietnamese fought as guerrilla fighters against the Japanese. American agents gave some guns to the Vietnamese fighters. The people of Vietnam had long wanted independence from the French, and in past years they had risen up several times in rebellion. Nationalism was now in the wind, as victory in World War II was in sight. Vietnamese leaders of the freedom movement who had left the country now returned and fought alongside their people. The first among those leaders was a man named Ho Chi Minh.

Vietnam's George Washington

The greatest patriot of his country is the man we know as Ho Chi Minh (1890–1969). He was born in central Vietnam in 1890, with the name Nguyen Sinh Cung. (Nguyen is a family name very common in Vietnam.) He attended a French high school, then worked as a deckhand on liners for three years. He visited American ports. He ended up in Paris during World War I, working at menial jobs, and joined radical groups that believed in independence for the colonies.

Then Ho Chi Minh (the name he took as a radical, meaning "He Who Enlightens") turned to the Communist party because it had a stronger position on colonial freedom. He went to Moscow and to China, where young Vietnamese came to study with him. As an exile, he organized the Indochinese Communist party.

In February 1941, Ho Chi Minh crossed the South China border into Japanese-occupied Vietnam. He organized the "Viet Minh," which stands for the Vietnamese Independence Brotherhood League. Ho said that its task was to "overthrow the Japanese and French and their jackals in Vietnam." He wanted to rid his country of all foreign influence, but he also wanted to help the Allies against Japan. At the end of the war, he led his followers into Hanoi and proclaimed an independent Vietnam. Ho used our Declaration of Independence as his model and asked for American aid. None came, and the Viet Minh went ahead on their own.

THE FRENCH SEEK TO REGAIN INDOCHINA

After World War II, the French wanted to regain control over Indochina. Great Britain recognized India's independence in 1947, but the French could not give up their valuable holdings in Southeast Asia. France offered the three countries membership in the French Union, organized in an attempt to keep its overseas territories. Cambodia and Laos agreed to join, but the Viet Minh held out for full independence.

In 1946, fighting broke out between French troops and Vietnamese. French warships shelled the city of Haiphong and killed 6,000 civilians. In the meantime, the French brought Bao Dai back as the head of state, hoping for popular support. Instead, a bloody guerrilla war went on for eight years. Because the Viet Minh stood for communism, which the United States dreaded, Washington gave heavy financial aid to the French and the Bao Dai regime.

Dien Bien Phu   The struggle was at a standstill in 1954. The French army had a base at Dien Bien Phu, north of Hanoi and near the Laos border. It was surrounded by Viet Minh soldiers under the command of General Vo Nguyen Giap, the ablest soldier of the post–World War II era. The Viet Minh closed in, and after President Eisenhower refused to send American aid, Giap's strategy brought the French to defeat in May. The defeat at Dien Bien Phu was a disaster for the French and effectively marked the end of their presence in Vietnam.

The Geneva Conference   In summer 1954 the concerned governments met at Geneva, Switzerland. An armistice was signed between the French Union and the Viet Minh. Vietnam was temporarily divided at the 17th Parallel, and a narrow demilitarized zone (DMZ) was set off, awaiting an election to decide between the Bao Dai and Ho Chi Minh governments.

The Vietnam War, 1965–1975

The election to decide on a government for a united Vietnam was never held. In late 1954 nearly 1 million Catholic and ethnic Chinese refugees from the north poured south, because the Viet Minh government was opposed to all forms of religion. The United States had to begin giving aid to the South, both food and military. Many U.S. military advisers were sent to help train the South Vietnam army. Bao Dai appointed as prime minister a Catholic, Ngo Dinh Diem, who then abolished the throne and became president. Bao Dai went into exile. While Ho Chi Minh called for national elections, Diem refused because he and the Americans feared the Viet Minh would win. Corruption, dictatorial ways, and anti-Buddhist actions weakened his government. In 1963, with silent U.S. approval, Diem's own generals rose against him and he was killed. The generals took over, but matters did not improve.

More and more U.S. military "advisers" were sent to South Vietnam after 1965. At its peak, the U.S. military strength in Vietnam was about a half million troops.

THE VIET CONG

In the jungle country of South Vietnam were guerrilla fighters called "Viet Cong," allies of the Viet Minh, as well as northern troops under General Giap. Supplies reached the Viet Cong from the north by way of the Ho Chi Minh Trail, a crude roadway through the forests of southeastern Laos. The American Central Intelligence Agency (CIA) recruited Hmong men and women to disrupt traffic on the trail. Thousands of the Hmong people were killed. The United States dropped countless bombs on Viet Cong hiding places in Laos and Cambodia. Another group in the southern Vietnam mountains, the Montagnards, were also recruited to harass the Viet Cong. The continual fighting and bombing created refugees from the countryside who flocked to the cities. Though the United States poured in massive funds, there was widespread hunger and unrest.

THE TET OFFENSIVE

In late January or early February the Vietnamese of all faiths celebrated their New Year, called "Tet," and a truce was customary. In 1968, however, General Giap surprised the South Vietnamese during Tet with a mass offensive against every town, including Saigon. The important city of Hue remained under siege for a month. Loss of lives on both sides was tremendous.

American support of the war was beginning to falter. At home, protests were rising. Thousands of young men refused to serve in the armed forces, and there were antiwar demonstrations. The U.S. government began to heed public feeling, and in 1969 the withdrawal of American troops slowly began. The same year, Ho Chi Minh died in Hanoi after a long illness. His successors swore to continue fighting until the Americans were driven out.

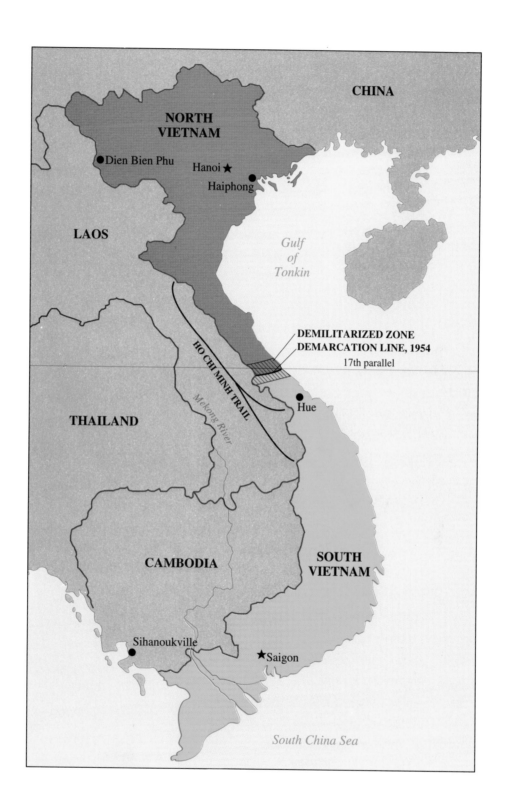

CHINA

NORTH
VIETNAM

●Dien Bien Phu

Hanoi ★
Haiphong

LAOS

*Gulf
of
Tonkin*

DEMILITARIZED ZONE
DEMARCATION LINE, 1954
17th parallel

HO CHI MINH TRAIL

Mekong River

THAILAND

●Hue

CAMBODIA

SOUTH
VIETNAM

Sihanoukville

★Saigon

South China Sea

Bao Dai

Born in 1913, he grew up in France, where he lived a frivolous life. From 1932 to 1945 he was emperor of Annam, a part of present Vietnam, and cooperated with the Vichy French and the Japanese. When the Viet Minh took over, he abdicated and became a citizen who served as an adviser to Ho Chi Minh's government. He went back to France; then in 1949 he returned as head of state of Vietnam. Diem ousted him and he went into exile.

Ngo Dinh Diem

He belonged to an important Roman Catholic family. Though an official under the French, he was a staunch nationalist. In 1954 he unwillingly became prime minister under Bao Dai. Corruption and his unfair favoring of his family and Roman Catholics over Buddhists caused the end of his regime and brought about his assassination.

Vo Nguyen Giap

Born in 1912 to a peasant family of central Vietnam, he became a Communist in the 1930s. Ho Chi Minh called him to China to become his chief aide. Giap organized the Viet Minh and became its leader in fighting the Japanese and the French. As commander in chief, he masterminded the victory at Dien Bien Phu and the Tet offensive. Though professionally untrained, he beat the best French and American generals. Retired now in Hanoi, he is considered one of the world's great military strategists.

Prince Norodom Sihanouk

He was born in 1922 and educated in Saigon and Paris. Sihanouk showed himself a man of contradictions. The French made him king of Cambodia in 1941, only to find that he favored independence. When France took over after World War II, he was in and out of Cambodia, and later head of an independent government favoring neutrality. Yet he allowed supplies for the Viet Minh to come through Cambodia's port, Sihanoukville. In 1965 he broke relations with the United States because of the bombings of his country. At one point he allied himself with the Khmer Rouge, and later he led a non-Communist party.

Lon Nol

He was a Cambodian general who served under Sihanouk. He became prime minister, overthrew Sihanouk, and led an anti-Communist government with American backing. When he failed to turn back the Communists, called the "Khmer Rouge," he escaped and found refuge in the United States, where he died.

Pol Pot

Born around 1926 as Saloth Sar in a peasant family of central Cambodia, he was a Buddhist monk until he became a Communist. He studied in Paris and returned to Cambodia in 1953. At that time he took Pol Pot as his name. As the leader of the Khmer Rouge, he used the most cruel means to transform Cambodia (Kampuchea) into a self-sufficient Communist country. After the Vietnamese took over in 1979, Pol Pot disappeared into the jungles of north Cambodia, where it is said he has a luxurious hideaway. He has rarely allowed himself to be photographed.

PEACE

Despite troop withdrawals and the first peace discussions in Paris, fighting continued between the two Vietnams. There was heavy bombing of Cambodia and of North Vietnam even at Christmas 1972. A month later, a peace agreement was signed by North and South Vietnam and the United States. American troops were brought home, prisoners of war were exchanged, and fighting was supposed to end. But North Vietnam and South Vietnam continued the struggle. On April 30, 1975, Saigon fell to the North Vietnamese and Viet Cong forces.

THE HUMAN LOSSES

The United States suffered nearly 60,000 dead and missing in action. More than 200,000 South Vietnamese soldiers were killed, and about a half million civilians. As for the North Vietnamese, it is believed that a million soldiers died, and the number of civilian deaths is unknown. The death toll in Laos and Cambodia during the war cannot be guessed. An estimate is several hundred thousand. The total dead in the Vietnam War has been estimated at 4 million, and the total cost at $500 billion.

In Laos, the U.S. planes bombed not only the Ho Chi Minh Trail but the northern strongholds of the Pathet Lao, who were allies of the Viet Minh. Many were killed, and many fled the country after the war, when the Pathet Lao took over.

Peace in Vietnam did not mean peace for Cambodia. Prince Norodom Sihanouk, the hereditary ruler, had been forced out by Lon Nol, who had U.S. support. Sihanouk formed an alliance with Pol Pot, leader of the Khmer Rouge. The result was a bloody civil war between the Khmer Rouge and Lon Nol's government in which many thousands died.

THE BOAT PEOPLE

During spring 1975, as the North Vietnamese pushed southward, people were in panic to escape ahead of the troops. In the coastal cities, South Vietnamese soldiers with their families, ethnic Chinese, and Catholic civilians fought to get onto boats. Women and children were trampled. In Saigon, influential persons paid anything to get out. The remaining U.S. officials took a relative few of them on helicopters. The United States arranged for many people to go by ship to refugee camps in the Philippines and Guam. Thousands of others piled onto boats of any kind. These "boat people" continued over the years to flee from Communist Vietnam, hoping to reach safe harbor in China, Thailand, Malaysia, Indonesia, or Hong Kong.

The Ordeal of the Boat People

A group of Vietnamese who had escaped in a small boat headed for Thailand were boarded by pirates.

"The pirates tied up some of the Vietnamese men and threw them into the water. The remaining people were tied up too, and locked in the hold after being stripped of their belongings. After this, the pirates began . . . to pillage and rape people. One person was killed after being dealt a blow with an iron bar. Another had his finger cut off because he was unable to pull off his wedding ring. When everything was looted, the pirates . . . released the people in the hold and kicked them back to our boat. Some fell into the water and drowned with their hands bound behind their backs."

Source: Adapted from Bruce Grant, *The Boat People* (New York: Penguin, 1979), p. 66.

THE KILLING FIELDS

The Khmer Rouge under Pol Pot killed as many as a million of a population of about 6 million Cambodians. The Khmer Rouge killed its own people in the effort to change the country. Intellectuals and professionals were marked out for murder, along with anyone suspected of being against the regime. The soldiers, often teenagers, drilled to serve Pol Pot, killed people on a mere whim. The tragic locations of the executions came to be called the "Killing Fields," and this title was given to a motion picture that told the true story of a man who was caught up in these terrible events.

Dith Pran was born in 1942. A Buddhist, he grew up at Siem Reap, near the Angkor temples, where he worked as a guide and interpreter. He had a good education, learned English, and had a wife and children. In the 1970s Pran began working for the *New York Times* office in Phnom Penh. He was assigned to a journalist, Sydney H. Schanberg, who was covering the war between the Khmer Rouge and the U.S.-supported government of Lon Nol. They became close friends.

On April 12, 1975, the Khmer Rouge were closing in on Phnom Penh. American officials and newsmen were being flown out in helicopters. Pran's family was sent out to safety. They reached the United States as refugees. Schanberg was able to get to Thailand and then home. Pran went into the country, disguised as a farm worker.

For more than four years, Pran managed to evade discovery and death by the Khmer Rouge. He had many narrow escapes, he nearly starved to death, and he saw countless horrible sights. In 1978 the Vietnamese army invaded Kampuchea, as Pol Pot had renamed it, and drove the Khmer Rouge to the jungles. Pran managed to escape to Thailand and later to a reunion with his family in San Francisco and with Schanberg. The story of his experience, written by Schanberg, became the movie *The Killing Fields*.

Dith Pran (1942–)

Dith Pran became a photographer for the *New York Times* and now lives in Brooklyn with his wife and children. In 1989, he revisited Cambodia as a member of a human rights organization, invited by Hun Sen, the Cambodian prime minister. Pran wrote the story of that visit himself. He and other members held a Buddhist ceremony in memory of Pol Pot's victims. They took two turtles to a nearby field and freed them. "Freeing turtles is part of an old tradition," Pran wrote. "By giving freedom to another living creature we gain merit and release from suffering, for ourselves or for the people we love, in the life to come."[1]

[1]*Source: New York Times Magazine,* September 24, 1989, p. 54.

The Refugees Come to America

The people we call "refugees" are different from "regular" immigrants to the United States. They did not plan on coming here. The majority of immigrants, before the 1970s, came of their free will, looking for the better life they had heard of. They were "pulled" to this country. But refugees are "pushed" to leave their homelands by fear of persecution and worse.

THE FIRST WAVE

The 1975 refugees were called the *first wave* of people who fled their homeland as a direct result of the Vietnam War. The Southeast Asian refugees have gone not only to the United States. They have also gone to Hong Kong, Canada, Europe, and Australia. But most of them have come to America, which is seen as a land of promise. Also, the United States has been more willing to accept many refugees. It is part of a tradition. And some Americans feel that they owe it to the refugees, whose plight is a result of U.S. actions in Southeast Asia.

Before the fall of Saigon (which was renamed Ho Chi Minh City) in 1975, many people from South Vietnam were already in the United States. They included college students, government and business officials, and people brought here for technical and military training. So they were stranded. They became *asylees:* that is, they were granted *asylum,* a word meaning "a safe refuge." When asylees apply for admission, they are in the United States or at a port of entry; refugees are overseas.

The first wave to leave Vietnam included many who were considered "high-risk" cases. They included ethnic Chinese, members of the Catholic elite (as well as Catholics who had come south earlier as refugees from Hanoi), army officers, government officials, teachers, and employees of American firms. Some of these had left even before the North Vietnamese took over because they saw what was coming. Most of the first-wave refugees were well educated and came in family groups. More than half were Catholics. Some were less prosperous people, such as farmers and fishermen.

There were extremes of fortune among these refugees. Some left with lots of money, others fled with hardly more than the clothes on their backs. By the end of 1975, about 130,000 refugees had left Vietnam. They included 4,000 orphans; many were Amerasians, the children of U.S. servicemen and Vietnamese mothers.

A Vietnamese family at a temporary receiving station in the Philippines

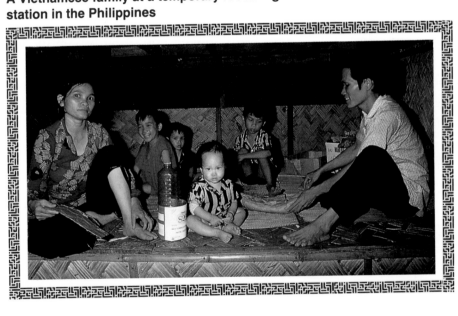

U.S. Immigration Policy

America did not always welcome people from Asia. There were no immigration laws until 1882, when the Chinese Exclusion Act was passed to keep out Chinese labor. A broader law, the National Origins Act of 1924, barred natives of any part of Asia. Quotas (limited numbers) were established for such countries as Great Britain and Germany. During World War II, when China was one of the Allies, the Chinese Exclusion Act was repealed. A quota of 105 Chinese per year was set. But there was still no policy for refugees as such. The only way that people fleeing from ill treatment could come into the United States was under the quotas.

The McCarran-Walter Act in 1952 did away with race as a barrier. It also allowed the government to admit "parolees," persons in a desperate situation, and this worked for some of the refugees. Refugees were first recognized by the Refugee Relief Act of 1953, which approved admitting 205,000 nonquota persons, but only until 1957. The 1965 Immigration Act made the rules even more liberal. It set a target of 120,000 per year from the Western Hemisphere and 170,000 from the Eastern Hemisphere. But since family members of persons already in America did not count, and because exceptions were made for refugees and asylees, in some years more than 800,000 were let in.

We should note that the United Nations is also concerned with refugees. The Office of the High Commissioner for Refugees, established in 1951, works with governments and volunteer agencies ("Volags") and helps to raise funds for their work.

HELP FOR THE REFUGEES

In April 1975, it was clear that South Vietnam would be taken over by the North. U.S. president Gerald R. Ford set up a special interagency task force to help people get safely out of Vietnam and resettled. About 130,000 people went to temporary receiving stations in the Philippines, Guam, and Hawaii. For several weeks, the refugees went to English as a Second Language (ESL) classes and got some knowledge of life in the United States. Others stayed in "first asylum" camps in Thailand and Malaysia until they could be sent to the United States or other countries. The stations and camps were under the United Nations, but the United States provided most of the funds.

There was no question that these refugees were entitled to assistance and entrance into the United States, but as "parolees." When President Jimmy Carter signed the Refugee Assistance Act in 1980, the United States finally had a refugee policy on paper. The act created a permanent Refugee Resettlement Program. It set a higher number of refugees who could be admitted. The president could raise the number even more, with the agreement of Congress. The states were given power to deal with refugees, and federal funds were provided. A system of priorities was created. The status of an asylee was made official. By 1980, the United States had accepted some 400,000 refugees from Southeast Asia, mostly from Vietnam.

Who Is a Refugee?

A person outside his or her country of nationality who is unable or unwilling to return to that country because of persecution or a well-founded fear of persecution on account of race, religion, nationality, membership in a particular social group, or political opinion.

Source: The Refugee Assistance Act, 1980.

In fewer words, a refugee is a person who flees his or her native country for safety in a time of distress. However, in recent years, the United States has routinely denied refugee status to Haitians, Salvadoreans, Chileans, and others.

THE RECEPTION CENTERS

The majority of the first-wave refugees were then flown to one of four reception centers in the United States (see p. 35). They stayed in tents or barracks, divided up by low partitions so that family groups could be together. Each refugee was given bed linens, toilet articles, a meal ticket, and camp number. There was not much privacy. Everybody shared toilets and ate together in mess halls. Records were kept on education, work experience, religion, and so on, and each person got a medical examination and a social security number. The head of each household was registered with a volunteer social service agency. The task of the volunteer agency, or Volag, was to look after the refugees' welfare and help find sponsors and jobs once people left the centers.

Life in the centers was not easy. American ways were confusing to most refugees. And people were anxious, bored,

A U.S. reception center for refugees

and unhappy. There was not enough understanding of such problems on the part of the social workers. As sympathetic as the social workers were, their background in the culture of the different Southeast Asian peoples was often inadequate. The idea was to help people give up their customs and adopt "American" ones. That policy went against the traditions of the Southeast Asians and caused even more worries.

PREPARING FOR LIFE IN THE UNITED STATES

Despite some problems, life in the centers could be constructive. There was schooling for children from six to eighteen years old. Grown-ups had classes in English and job training. People were taught how to shop, apply for a job, rent an apartment in an American town, and so on. There were recreation programs with movies and volleyball games, which the youngsters were quick to learn. One camp had a newspaper that explained camp rules and American life.

On the other hand, language continued to be a problem. There were few social workers who knew the refugees' languages, and everything had to be done in English. In some camps, the native language was forbidden in the classroom. The students did not respond, and this was discouraging on both sides. But it was of great importance for the newcomers to learn English in order to get along.

The average stay of refugees at the centers was seven months. By December 1975, all the first-wave refugees had left the centers. About 8,000 who each had at least $4,000 were released to make their way on their own. About 122,000 found sponsors. Some families stayed near the centers because they had found friends or sponsors nearby.

The sponsors could be churches, organizations, companies or other employers, farmers, families, and other individuals.

Sometimes a volunteer agency would act as the sponsor—for example, when an especially close relationship with a refugee family had started at the center. Unfortunately, there were cases of abuse by sponsors. A farmer would sponsor a refugee family in order to put them to work, then would fail to pay the promised wages or provide decent housing. The agency would then try to help out.

The Reception Centers in The United States

Camp Pendleton, between San Diego and Los Angeles, California
Fort Indiantown Gap, east of Harrisburg, Pennsylvania
Fort Chaffee, near Fort Smith, Arkansas
Eglin Air Force Base, east of Pensacola, Florida

Major Volunteer Agencies (VOLAGS)

American Council of Nationality Services (ACNS)
American Fund for Czechoslovak Refugees (AFCR)
American Red Cross
Church World Services (CWS)
Hebrew Immigrant Aid Society (HIAS)
International Rescue Committee (IRC)
Lutheran Immigration and Refugee Services (LIRS)
Tolstoy Foundation
Traveler's Aid International Social Services
United States Catholic Conference (USCC)

REFUGEES AFTER 1975

The first wave of refugees in 1975 was made up chiefly of Vietnamese, including ethnic Chinese. For several years after that time there was a decline in the number who came to this country. But, starting in 1980, there was a sharp increase, and this was known as the *second wave*. This was caused by several different factors. The 1980 Refugee Act allowed many more to come in, and there *were* many more who were desperate to get to the United States. The violence in Laos and Cambodia drove thousands to the camps of first asylum in Thailand, Indonesia, and the Philippines. There were many more boat people trying to reach the camps.

The United States first agreed to accept 7,000 refugees from the camps per month, then doubled this to 14,000. From October 1979 to September 1980, over 166,000 Southeast Asian refugees were admitted, and 70,000 of these were not from Vietnam. Altogether, from 1975 to 1984, more than 700,000 came to the United States from Vietnam, Laos, and Cambodia.

Almost as many refugees went to other countries. Their placement was handled by the United Nations. By the end of 1981, China had taken a quarter of a million, France and Canada more than 80,000 each, Australia about 60,000, West Germany 20,000, and Great Britain 16,000. About 200,000 remained in Thailand, the main country of first asylum.

The following "pie charts" show how the proportion of legal immigrants to this country changed from the 1930s to the mid-1980s. The effect of the changes in immigration laws in the 1960s is clear to see. So is the effect of the sudden arrival of Southeast Asian refugees in the 1970s, and the second wave after that. As of 1985, the Asian American population of the United States was about 5 million and growing fast, including people from the other countries of east and south Asia.

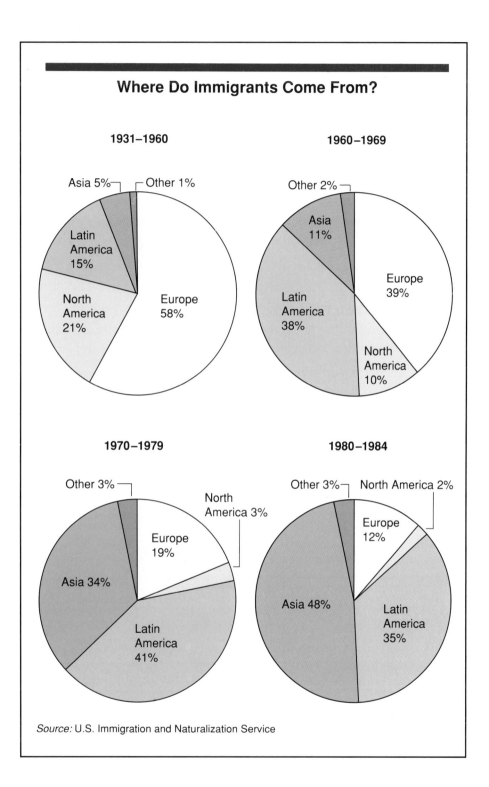

Where Do Immigrants Come From?

1931–1960

Asia 5%
Other 1%
Latin America 15%
North America 21%
Europe 58%

1960–1969

Other 2%
Asia 11%
Europe 39%
Latin America 38%
North America 10%

1970–1979

Other 3%
North America 3%
Europe 19%
Asia 34%
Latin America 41%

1980–1984

Other 3%
North America 2%
Europe 12%
Asia 48%
Latin America 35%

Source: U.S. Immigration and Naturalization Service

Most of the second-wave refugees have been uneducated people—farmers, laborers, fishermen. They are even less likely to know English or, for that matter, to be able to read and write their own language. The reception centers no longer exist, and federal and state funds are not so plentiful. The volunteer agencies take responsibility for these refugees while they are still in the asylum camps. They often search the camps for relatives of refugees who are already in America.

The people in the refugee camps include Vietnamese who came in boats. It is estimated that about half of the boat people lost their lives on the sea. A larger number of refugees came over land into Thailand from Cambodia during the bad times of Pol Pot and afterward when the Vietnamese invaded their country. The Hmong, fleeing the Pathet Lao and the Vietnamese, came over the Mekong River into Thailand. As late as 1983, nearly 60,000 Hmong and 15,000 lowland Lao were waiting in the Thai camps, right next door.

A Vietnamese refugee said in an interview: "My life in the camp was terrible. The Thai officers treated us like animals. They were inhuman." And another said: "It was little more than a prison camp, crowded with more than one hundred thousand people living in terrible conditions without enough food, medical services, and shelter and no recreation or teaching. The Thai government threatened to force us back to our homeland because we were a burden on them." Later, for training before going to the United States, this refugee was sent to a camp in Indonesia. "There we were well prepared to get ready for the adjustments to the new life in America. . . . I took the ESL classes and for days and nights studied and practiced the new language."[1]

[1]Source: Adapted from N. Caplan, J. K. Whitmore, and M. H. Choy, *The Boat People and Achievement in America* (Ann Arbor: Univ. of Michigan Press, 1989), p. 13.

A young Vietnamese refugee receives medical
assistance (top) and a Laotian family has a
resettlement interview at an asylum camp in
Thailand (bottom).

Settling Into American Life

As we have seen, the Southeast Asian Americans are a highly diverse population. Not only do they come from three very different countries, but they include a wide range of people, representing different histories, religions, clans, languages, and political beliefs. They include people unable to read, college students, families on welfare, people in business who are successful, farmers and fishermen, priests and nuns, members of gangs.

But these Southeast Asian refugees share experiences that not all other Asian and European immigrants have known. They were uprooted by war and violence. Many went through cruel invasions, dangerous sea journeys, and refugee camps. Many lost families and everything they owned. They came to a country they knew little or nothing about and never expected to see. They had never dreamed of being immigrants. And, before 1952, they could not even have been accepted as immigrants to the United States of America.

COMMON CONCERNS

As the table on the facing page shows, many ethnic groups exist among the nationalities of the refugees. In spite of their differences, all Southeast Asian Americans share several concerns and problems that may affect how they fit into life in this country.

Goals   Some of the refugees must decide whether to accept a future as Americans, or whether to hope eventually to go home. Many are coming to realize that they can keep some of their old customs and still fit into American life.

Sticking Together   There are advantages for the refugees to keep their families and clans together and live in groups. Earlier immigrants had done this also. This gives them support in important ways, including their businesses. At first, this was not understood by many other Americans.

The Role of Government and the Volags   Sometimes the work of the volunteer agencies was not well planned. They were not always sensitive to the feelings of people and were too eager to force the refugees to take up "American" ways.

Attitudes of the "Host Society"   There is not so much prejudice toward Asians as there used to be, but it still exists. In some places, the refugees continue to encounter unfriendliness and a lack of sympathy and understanding.

Ethnic Identity   Asian Americans can be readily recognized by their appearance, and they can't merge into American society as easily as people of European descent.

Work and Education   The great majority of the refugees started out with the language barrier, which made it hard to find jobs and continue education. Even when they learned English, it was a problem to find child care while they went to work or school. And many have had to accept positions at a lower level than those they held in their homeland.

Some Ethnic Groups Among the Refugees

From Vietnam	From Cambodia	From Laos
Vietnamese	Khmer	Lowland Lao
Tonkinese	(Cambodians)	Hmong
Annamese	Mi Khmer	Vietnamese
Cham	Krom	Thai
Montagnards	Vietnamese	Mon-Kher
Khmer	Malay	Yao
(Cambodians)	Cham	Nung
Hmong	Cham-Malay	Man
Tai	Thai	Mien
Chinese	Chinese	Khmu
		Chinese

Cambodian Americans gather together for Buddhist worship.

THE VIETNAMESE

People from Vietnam form the largest group of refugees from Southeast Asia. There are about 700,000 in the United States, among the million refugees who have arrived. Among them are many ethnic Chinese whose families have lived in Vietnam for generations. This difference presents a slight problem to the U.S. Census Bureau when it tries to count people by their ancestry. In any case, the ethnic Chinese from Southeast Asia usually find their way to the Chinatowns in our cities or to other communities of Chinese. Chinese refugee families are more likely to have relatives and friends already settled in the United States.

Before the Vietnam War, there were probably not more than a few hundred Vietnamese in this country. Most of these were students, diplomatic personnel, and businesspeople from South Vietnam. They were among the group who were stranded by the war and were granted asylum.

The better-educated, better-connected, and more Western-ized Vietnamese who arrived in the first wave of refugees have tended to find their way on their own.

Religious leaders among the refugees, such as Buddhist and Catholic priests and nuns, have carried on their work with their people. Some have become social workers, helping other refugees. As the Buddhists get together and find the funds, they build temples where there are enough worshipers.

After the Fighting   The Vietnamese in the second wave are people who failed to escape in 1975 and who have found life under the Communists impossible to bear. The new government intended to rebuild society. Businesses were taken over. "Reeducation camps" were started for people who were involved with the former regime. Thousands, especially business and professional people in the cities, with their families, were ordered to go to the country, where "new economic zones" had been created. They had to do unfamiliar hard work—dig irrigation canals, build roads, work in the fields. These are some of the people who risked their lives as boat people and also lost their lives. Others who had some money got out by means of the "big boat trade." This was a racket, charging high fares in gold to transport people to China and elsewhere in rickety old freighters. Government officials, it is said, connived in that traffic in an attempt to get rid of the ethnic Chinese.

In 1979, the Vietnam government and the United Nations agreed on the "Orderly Departure Program." Under that program, refugees get exit visas to leave Vietnam and resettle wherever they can be admitted. The next year, the government started releasing inmates of the labor camps and reeducation centers and allowing them to emigrate.

Poem of the Boat People

Can you imagine human hair
Flowing all over the sea,
Children's bodies ready to dissolve
As human meat dinners of fish?

But they keep on leaving
As humanity turn their heads away
And still they serenely
Throw themselves into death.

Source: A poem by Du Tu Le, as quoted in a Vietnamese American magazine, *Dat Moi,* April 1979.

The New Year Holidays   In the countries of Southeast Asia, including Vietnam, the New Year is celebrated at the time of the full moon just before the spring planting. This is called the "lunar new year." It is a three-day festival, which may fall in late January or February. The Vietnamese call it "Tet." It is a survival of old Chinese beliefs, and it probably originated to ensure a good harvest.

Everyone celebrates Tet, whether Buddhist, Catholic, or Confucian. A few days before, shops become crowded with people buying presents for their family and friends. The streets are ablaze with colored lanterns and decorated booths. On the eve of Tet, Buddhist families may come together before an altar. They pray for the spirits of their ancestors and invite them to their holiday festivities. They also ask forgiveness for mistakes and pay back their debts. Outside, fireworks and firecrackers are set off. In homes, peach blossoms are cut and put in a vase. Decorations of gold and red paper are put up everywhere. Children receive money in red envelopes. Food is sacrificed, and there are also special dishes that are cooked and eaten. It is the most important holiday of the year. It is said that whatever happens on that day foretells what will happen in people's lives for the coming year.

Vietnamese Americans also celebrate the Tet holidays. In San Jose, California, for example, the entire Santa Clara fairground is given over to the Tet festivities. They exchange gifts and visits and eat festive meals, to which American treats are sometimes added. If a priest or a nun of the family's faith is nearby, he or she comes and performs traditional religious ceremonies. The Tet celebration is a link with the life in the homeland.

The Catholics from Vietnam, besides celebrating Tet, observe Christmas, Easter, and other holidays of the Christian church.

Vietnamese American students performing during
a Tet celebration at a school in Biloxi, Mississippi

Where the Vietnamese Live   When the refugees arrived at the reception centers, and afterward in the second wave, they were placed with sponsors scattered widely around the United States. The intention was to break up the large family and clan groups and encourage the newcomers to mix with their neighbors. In this way, instead of preserving the ways of the homeland, the Vietnamese would be encouraged to become American all the more quickly.

This proved to be a mistake. A single Vietnamese family in a small town or a city neighborhood felt lonely and unhappy. The language problem made the situation even worse. Even when the sponsor was kind and thoughtful, the Vietnamese family missed the companionship of their own kind. So gradually most Vietnamese moved to places where others had begun to form a community. In this way, large settlements of Vietnamese sprang up in certain places. Often, families and clan groups that had been separated were reunited.

And yet, by now there are Vietnamese in nearly every one of the states. Many families have stayed close to their original sponsors because of a good relationship. In some cases, they found work they liked and wanted to stay with it.

The greatest concentrations are in California. There are large Vietnamese communities in Orange County, in Los Angeles, in the neighborhood of San Jose, and in San Diego. Others are in New York, the area around Washington, D.C., Minneapolis, and along the coast of the Gulf of Mexico from Florida to Texas.

Orange County   Some Vietnamese who landed in the refugee center at Camp Pendleton, California, found sponsors nearby in Anaheim and other towns of Orange County. So they stayed. And other families came, some moving across the country to join relatives and friends. One of the largest Vietnamese settlements is called Little Saigon, in Garden Grove, California. There are Vietnamese noodle shops, mar-

This supermarket helps serve the large Vietnamese
American community in San Jose, California.

kets selling Vietnamese groceries, Chinese shops selling herbal medicines, gift shops, offices of Vietnamese professionals, and clubs where Vietnamese music can be heard. Little Saigon gives the refugees a place where they can speak their language and feel almost as if in their homeland.

San Jose   Santa Clara County, California, has the third-largest population of Southeast Asian refugees in the United States. In 1988 their number was estimated at 100,000, and at least 75,000 were from Vietnam. The Vietnamese took over a shabby downtown business section and transformed it into a busy shopping center, with Vietnamese shops and markets, and offices for doctors, dentists, and lawyers. There are restaurants, real estate and insurance agencies, travel agencies, acupuncture clinics, automobile service stations, and a Vietnamese Chamber of Commerce. Many Vietnamese, both men and women, work at assembly-line jobs in the "Silicon Valley" high-tech companies nearby. Less than 15 percent of the families received welfare, and most of these were new refugees, who were entitled to eighteen months of assistance after their arrival. Taxes paid by the Vietnamese citizens are greater than the cost of welfare for the new arrivals.

Vietnamese children quickly overcome the language barrier and do well in school. In the graduating class of one California high school, out of eleven honor students, seven were Vietnamese.

Problems That Continue   There are still many problems for the Vietnamese Americans and others from Southeast Asia. Many families still have incomes below the poverty line.

For the elderly, life can be difficult. They have not been as quick to learn English and the new ways of living, and often they are lonely. They see their children taking up American life-styles which are so different. In the homeland, parents and older people were shown respect and obedience. Parents had to be asked their permission for marriage. Now there is sometimes misunderstanding between parents with their old-country views and their Americanized children. In some cities, the young people have formed gangs that get involved in crime. They even prey on their own people. They are often youths who had language and school problems, who couldn't find work. Unfortunately, they take their gang models from American youth.

Often there is poor understanding on the part of Americans. Some think that the refugees take advantage of welfare and steal jobs. If a refugee's English is hard to understand, some people will criticize and insult him. There have been cases of outright abuse and cheating of refugees. Also, there is job rivalry. Many Vietnamese had been fishermen in the old country. They bought fishing boats at much sacrifice and set up business on the Gulf Coast. Some local fishermen were against any competition. They accused the Vietnamese of overfishing the grounds and using wrong techniques. The problems were eventually worked out between the fishermen. In one Texas town, the Ku Klux Klan made trouble.

Vietnamese American fishermen working on the Gulf Coast in Texas

A Vietnamese American Poet

Trung was born on an island off southern Vietnam. When he was sixteen, the Communists took over. He got in trouble for passing out anti-Communist leaflets. He knew he would be arrested, and he and some friends stole a boat and escaped. They ran out of food and water. Many ships passed them by. They landed in Thailand and stayed for months in a refugee camp. At last, a brother-in-law in San Jose agreed to be Trung's sponsor. Trung flew to the United States and moved into a slum apartment with the brother-in-law and other young men from his hometown. In high school he found math easy but English difficult. Trung was attacked by a gang of boys, who said, "Hey, man, get out of America!" They stabbed him, and he was taken to the hospital. After he got well, his social worker discovered that Trung had been writing poems since he was thirteen. "When I feel sad and lonely," Trung said, "I write poems or I play the guitar." Here is part of one of Trung's poems in translation.

I Miss You, O Vietnam

When the autumn afternoon came and the autumn breeze
    gently blew,
I gazed in astonishment at the leaves of grass swaying
    slowly.
And gloomily I recalled the good old time
Which was being shut off and gradually wiped out from my
    mind.
I don't know whether my homeland is still existing.
With grief, I see months and days passing.
I miss you, O Vietnam, where rest generations of my
    ancestors.
I miss my small village stretching out amidst the ocean. . . .

Source: As quoted in J. A. Freeman, *Hearts of Sorrow: Vietnamese-American Lives* (Palo Alto, Calif.: Stanford Univ. Press, 1989), pp. 420–421.

THE CAMBODIANS

The Khmers, or Cambodians, began to come to the United States in larger numbers as part of the second wave, only after 1979. Before 1979 the rigid controls of the Pol Pot regime prevented most chances to escape. Once the refugees got to the camps in Thailand, most were held there for long periods, sometimes years, before they were accepted by the United States and other countries. By now, more than 165,000 Khmer have found their way here. They include educated people as well as peasants who were starving. That is a small number compared to the many thousands killed by the Khmer Rouge.

The ethnic Chinese refugees from Cambodia tended to go to Chinatowns in the cities. Many settled in Monterey Park, east of Los Angeles.

In the early 1980s the U.S. government started a program to send Cambodian refugees in clusters to a dozen cities outside of California. At that time, few Cambodians had relatives in California. A great many of the refugees were unmarried people, who had lost their families in the killing fields. There were also many widowed people with children. These people were settled at one place in groups of from 300 to 1,200. And extended families among the Cambodians were not separated but sent together to one of the "cluster sites." This policy worked well, in that people seemed to be contented and not likely to move on to another place.

Larger settlements did come together, however. Long Beach, south of Los Angeles, is one of the most important. That city has Cambodian markets, shops, clubs, and a Buddhist temple. There are good numbers of Cambodians also in New York; Houston, Texas; Lowell, Massachusetts; and Washington, D.C.

Problems for the Khmers   Many of the Cambodians suffer from deep depression. The doctors call this a "posttraumatic stress disorder." In their homeland they went through terrible experiences of war and mass killings, which have left scars on their minds and spirits. A Cambodian boy told a social worker, "It hurts inside when I remember what happened. I try not to think about it, but I dream and see my brother who they killed. I dream they keep shooting him and shooting him until I wake up."[1]

The best help for such depressed people comes from the presence of friends and relatives and from their Buddhist religion. Many Cambodians dream of returning to their homeland, but they realize that there is little chance of that.

THE LAO AND THE HMONG

The refugees from Laos represent two distinct peoples, the Lao from the lowlands and the Hmong from the mountains. The Lao were split into the Pathet Lao, who are Communist, and the Royal Lao, who are not. During the 1970s the two sides were at war. The losers, the Royal Lao, fled to Thailand and eventually to the United States and elsewhere. As we have seen, the Hmong had helped the South Vietnamese and Americans during their war against the Viet Minh. With the victory of the North Vietnamese, the Hmong had good reason to fear their punishment.

The largest influx of Laotians was in 1980, when the more liberal Refugee Act was put into force. That year, 50,000 refugees came. The majority were Hmong and people from some of the other mountain tribes. It is estimated that more than 50,000 Hmong are now in this country. Because they are so different from other Southeast Asians, the Hmong have attracted a larger share of attention.

The Hmong come from what is called a "preliterate society." No alphabet had been created for their language until

[1]*Source:* As quoted in R. Takaki, *Strangers from a Different Shore* (Boston: Little, Brown, 1989), p. 469.

Dressed in traditional clothes, this Hmong family
poses on their front porch in California.

quite recent years. Life in their homeland was little touched by Western ways. Yet as farmers in the jungle clearings, many Hmong were well off. They had a rich culture. They have found it more difficult to adapt to American life than any of the other people from Southeast Asia. Many had to be taught to read in their own language before they could learn to read or speak English. And the technical side of American life—plumbing, electricity, telephones—was a mystery when they arrived here. But the Hmong have proved to be quick to learn.

Where the Hmong Settle   When the Hmong families first arrived in the United States, they were resettled throughout the country. But soon many began to move, following the pattern of their lives in the Laos mountains. They moved in search of better work, less costly housing, or more agreeable weather. Many went to California, and there is one of the largest Hmong communities in the farm country around Fresno. Oddly, many Hmong have settled in Minnesota, Wisconsin, and Montana, states with hard winters. Some groups moved because they suffered hostile treatment. Hmong in Philadelphia were getting along, marketing their beautiful needlework and other crafts, until they ran into trouble with unfriendly neighbors. Then most of the families moved away.

Another group were invited to Marion, a town in the Blue Ridge Mountains of North Carolina, by church people. More than 600 have gone there and have found work in factories and on farms. Others continue to join them.

Yet many Hmong have not been fortunate. They have the highest percentage of families on welfare. Many cling to their ancestral beliefs, worry about evil spirits, distrust modern medicine, and put their trust in their own *shamans* ("medicine men"). In trying to carry on their old lives, they sometimes come into conflict with American customs and laws. Sometimes they hunt and fish where they please and start to build on

This *paj ntaub*, or "flower cloth," by artist Blia Lor reflects Hmong artistry and design.

any land that seems vacant. In the old country, a young man who wants a bride goes and takes her. In the United States he might get arrested for kidnapping.

A tragic sickness strikes some Hmong men (and men in other refugee groups). The doctors call it Sudden Unexplained Death Syndrome (SUDS). A man, young or old, who seems healthy, dies in his sleep, or suddenly loses consciousness and then dies. Some experts believe it may come from the stress of "culture shock," but this would not explain all cases. Research has not gone far because the Hmong are opposed to an "autopsy" (an operation on the dead person in an attempt to find the cause of death). They believe that the spirit must leave the body to join its ancestors before rebirth, and if the body has been cut by an autopsy, the spirit is not free to leave the mutilated body.

SOUTHEAST ASIAN FOOD

As it is in other countries of Asia, rice is the mainstay of Vietnamese, Cambodian, and Laotian cooking. Each region grows the variety of short-grain rice that it prefers. A great deal of long-grain rice is grown in the United States, and the refugees eat it gladly as the basis of almost every meal. Seasoning with spices, herbs, and aromatic vegetables is equally important. These include chilies (hot peppers), garlic, onions, lemon grass, turmeric, cardamom, cinnamon, coriander (cilantro), cumin, ginger, curry powder, and tamarind.

Bamboo shoots, manioc (cassava), pumpkin, and the meat and milk of coconuts go into dishes. Two products of soybeans are staples: bean curd and soy sauce. Dried fish and shrimp are also used for seasoning. Fish, chicken, duck, and pork are favorites, beef less so. The Southeast Asians like to roast meats and vegetables on open grills, and they have taken to American barbecues.

A sampling of Southeast Asian dishes

In California and in big U.S. cities, all the typical ingredients are to be found in "Oriental" grocery stores. Since Americans have grown fond of foods from overseas, supermarkets carry almost everything. Even the tropical fruits the refugees ate in their homelands, such as papayas, guavas, and mangoes, are available.

A Vietnamese breakfast might consist of *pho*, which is chicken soup with noodles, onions, and bits of meat. At a meal, each person holds a small bowl or basket of rice. With chopsticks, each one mixes in pieces from a large bowl of stew, perhaps chicken, duck, or rabbit, in the middle of the table.

Cambodians like *ansamcheks*, rice cakes with banana centers, and *pong tea kon*, a special kind of duck egg. Laotians enjoy *lab*, which is ground meat heavily spiced. A favorite side dish is papaya mashed with tomatoes, limes, and chilies. Children love bamboo sticks stuffed with sweet sticky rice, red beans, and coconut milk. And everyone enjoys street food sold by vendors—noodles, tiny meatballs, fish cakes, grilled pork bits, and rice cakes.

PRESENT AND FUTURE

During one generation—about twenty years—more than 1 million people from Southeast Asia have become Americans. A very few think of returning to their homelands. Most of these are men who dream of taking up arms against the regimes they fled from. For some, such dreams keep them going.

The refugees have had to deal with a two-sided problem. The first problem has been shared by nearly all refugees over the years, and that is the burden of *surviving*. They must find shelter and work. They must learn to speak an unknown language. They must adjust to a vastly changed world in spite of poverty, prejudice, uncertainty, and "culture shock."

The second problem is dealing with the *loss* of so much of the past. Southeast Asian refugees have lost home, country, family, friends, work, social position, and belongings. Many have lost a sure sense of who they are.

All Americans should be able to understand why a refugee from Laos or Cambodia can be confused, depressed, and sometimes suicidal.

The thing of greatest value that the refugees have not lost is inside them. That is their treasure: skills, traditions, family and group loyalty, courage, hope.

And, as with all other immigrants in the past, the ease with which the refugees will find their way in the United States depends on the reaction of the Americans they meet. That includes other minorities, both Asian and non-Asian. Most Americans come to appreciate newcomers from various cultures and experiences. Because of their particular experiences, Southeast Asian refugees may find it difficult to adjust initially. But it is certain that the American mosaic will profit from their arrival, just as it has from so many others.

Young Cambodian Americans perform a traditional dance.

Sources

Beckett, Ian. *Southeast Asia: From 1945.* New York: Franklin Watts, 1987.

Bouvier, L. F., and R. W. Gardner. "Immigration to the U.S.: The Unfinished Story." *Population Bulletin,* 41:4 (Nov. 1986), vol. 41, no. 4, November 1986.

Canesso, C. *Cambodia.* New York: Chelsea House, 1989.

Caplan, N., J. K. Whitmore, and M. H. Choy. *The Boat People and Achievement in America.* Ann Arbor: Univ. of Michigan Press, 1989.

Cerquone, J. *Uncertain Harbors: The Plight of Vietnamese Boat People.* Issue Paper, U.S. Committee for Refugees, October 1987.

Daniels, Roger. *Coming to America: A History of Immigration and Ethnicity in American Life.* New York: HarperCollins, 1990.

Freeman, J. A. *Hearts of Sorrow: Vietnamese-American Lives.* Palo Alto, Calif.: Stanford Univ. Press, 1989.

Gardner, R. W., B. Robey, and P. C. Smith. "Asian Americans: Growth, Change, and Diversity." *Population Bulletin,* vol. 40, no. 4, October 1985.

Grant, R. *The Boat People.* New York: Penguin, 1979.

Kitano, H. H. L., and Roger Daniels. *Asian Americans: Emerging Minorities.* Englewood Cliffs, N.J.: Prentice-Hall, 1988.

Koral, April. *An Album of War Refugees.* New York: Franklin Watts, 1989.

Lawson, D. *An Album of the Vietnam War.* New York: Franklin Watts, 1986.

National Geographic Magazine (Washington, D.C.). May 1980, September 1981, October 1988.

Osbourne, Christine. *Southeast Asian Food and Drink.* New York: Bookwright Press, 1989.

Schanberg, S. H. *The Death and Life of Dith Pran.* New York: Viking, 1985.

Strand, P. J., and W. Jones, Jr. *Indochinese Refugees in America.* Durham, N.C.: Duke Univ. Press, 1985.

Takaki, R. *Strangers from a Different Shore: A History of Asian Americans.* Boston: Little, Brown, 1989.

Thernstrom, Stephan, ed. *Harvard Encyclopedia of American Ethnic Groups.* Cambridge, Mass.: Harvard Univ. Press, 1980.

Index